# RISE TO THE TOP: MASTER THE ART OF STRATEGIC SUCCESS

1. Introduction
2. Chapter 1: Understanding Strategic Success
3. Chapter 2: The Foundation of Strategy
4. Chapter 3: Cultivating a Strategic Mindset
5. Chapter 4: Crafting a Winning Strategy
6. Chapter 5: Execution: Turning Strategy into Action
7. Chapter 6: Measuring Success and Adapting
8. Chapter 7: Building a Strategic Team
9. Chapter 8: Navigating Challenges and Obstacles
10. Chapter 9: Future Trends in Strategic Success
11. Chapter 10: Personal Branding for Strategic Success
12. Conclusion: Your Path to Strategic Success

# INTRODUCTION

In today's fast-paced and ever-evolving world, the ability to navigate complex challenges and seize opportunities is more crucial than ever. We live in an age where strategic success is not merely a desirable trait but a necessity for personal and professional growth. Whether you're an entrepreneur, a corporate leader, or an individual seeking to enhance your career, understanding the art of strategy is the key to rising above the competition and making a lasting impact.

# WHAT IS STRATEGIC SUCCESS?

At its core, strategic success is about having a clear vision and the ability to execute it effectively. It involves setting meaningful goals, developing actionable plans, and continually adapting to changing circumstances. Imagine standing on the edge of a vast ocean, looking out at the horizon. That horizon represents your goals and aspirations—your vision for the future. But to reach that horizon, you need a sturdy ship, a well-charted course, and the skills to navigate through storms and calm waters alike. This book serves as your compass, guiding you through the complexities of strategic thinking and execution.

# THE IMPORTANCE OF STRATEGIC THINKING

Strategic thinking is the process of analysing situations, anticipating challenges, and crafting thoughtful solutions. It requires a blend of creativity and analytical skills, allowing you to look beyond the immediate and envision the long-term consequences of your actions. In a world where information is abundant and choices are overwhelming, strategic thinking enables you to filter out the noise and focus on what truly matters.

Consider a chess game, where each move can lead to victory or defeat. A strategic thinker carefully evaluates each option, weighing the potential outcomes before making a decision. This mindset can be applied to various aspects of life, whether you're leading a team, managing a project, or planning your career trajectory.

# WHY THIS BOOK MATTERS

"Rise to the Top: Master the Art of Strategic Success" is not just another self-help book filled with theories and jargon. It is a practical guide designed to help you cultivate the skills and mindset necessary to achieve your goals. Each chapter delves into different facets of strategic success, offering insights, real-world examples, and actionable homework assignments to reinforce your learning. This book is your partner on the journey toward becoming a more strategic thinker and effective leader.

# WHAT YOU WILL LEARN

Throughout this book, you will discover:

**Understanding Strategic Success**: A comprehensive look at what it means to be strategically successful and the key components that contribute to it.

**The Foundation of Strategy**: Core principles of strategy development, including how to analyse your environment and set clear, achievable objectives.

**Cultivating a Strategic Mindset**: The traits of strategic thinkers and how to develop a mindset that embraces creativity, innovation, and resilience.

**Crafting a Winning Strategy**: Steps to create an effective strategy, supported by case studies of successful leaders and organisations.

**Execution: Turning Strategy into Action**: The critical role of execution in strategy and how to develop actionable plans to achieve your goals.

**Measuring Success and Adapting**: Techniques for tracking your progress and adapting your strategy based on results and feedback.

**Building a Strategic Team**: The importance of collaboration and leadership styles in fostering a strategic culture.

**Navigating Challenges and Obstacles**: Identifying common challenges and building resilience to overcome them.

**Future Trends in Strategic Success**: Exploring emerging trends and technologies that shape the future of strategy.

**Personal Branding for Strategic Success**: The significance of personal branding in achieving strategic goals and practical steps for building your brand.

Each chapter builds on the previous one, creating a cohesive learning experience that empowers you to apply these principles in your own life. The homework assignments at the end of each chapter will encourage you to reflect on what you've learned and actively work on developing your strategic skills.

# YOUR JOURNEY BEGINS HERE

As you embark on this journey, remember that mastering the art of strategic success is not an overnight endeavour. It requires time, effort, and a willingness to learn from both successes and setbacks. Embrace the process and be open to growth.

Your goals may seem distant now, but with the right strategies and mindset, you can close the gap between where you are today and where you want to be. Each page of this book is a step toward unlocking your potential and achieving your dreams.

Welcome to "Rise to the Top: Master the Art of Strategic Success." Together, let's navigate the path to success, build a robust strategy, and rise to the challenges ahead. The journey is yours to embark upon—let's make it a remarkable one!

# CHAPTER 1: UNDERSTANDING STRATEGIC SUCCESS

Strategic success is a term that resonates deeply with anyone striving to achieve their goals, whether in business, personal endeavours, or life in general. But what does it truly mean? This chapter will unravel the concept of strategic success, delve into its essential components, and help you understand why it is crucial for achieving your ambitions.

# WHAT IS STRATEGIC SUCCESS?

At its essence, **strategic success** is about achieving your long-term goals through careful planning, execution, and continuous improvement. It involves not just reaching your destination but doing so in a way that is sustainable and meaningful. Strategic success is not a one-time event; rather, it is an ongoing process that requires regular assessment and adaptation.

Think of strategic success as a journey rather than a destination. When you embark on a road trip, you don't simply hop in your car and hope for the best. You plan your route, consider the stops you want to make, and prepare for potential detours along the way. In the same way, achieving strategic success involves setting a clear direction, anticipating challenges, and being ready to pivot when necessary.

# THE KEY COMPONENTS OF STRATEGIC SUCCESS

To fully grasp the concept of strategic success, it is essential to explore its key components. Each of these elements plays a vital role in shaping your path toward achieving your goals.

**Vision and Mission**
The first step toward strategic success is having a clear vision of where you want to go. Your vision is like a lighthouse guiding you through the fog, providing direction and purpose. It answers the question, "What do I want to achieve?" A strong vision is inspiring and motivates you to take action.

Alongside your vision, you need a mission statement. This is a more concrete declaration of your purpose, outlining how you plan to achieve your vision. It defines the "why" behind your actions and serves as a roadmap for your journey.

**Example:** If your vision is to create a healthier community, your mission might involve educating others about nutrition and wellness, organising fitness programs, and advocating for better food policies.

# SETTING GOALS AND OBJECTIVES

Once you have a clear vision and mission, the next step is to set specific, measurable goals. Goals give you something tangible to work toward and help you break down your vision into manageable pieces.

**Here's where the SMART criteria come into play:**

**Specific**: Clearly define what you want to achieve.

**Measurable**: Determine how you will measure progress.

**Achievable**: Ensure your goals are realistic and attainable.

**Relevant**: Align your goals with your overall vision and mission.

**Time-bound**: Set deadlines for your goals to create a sense of urgency.

**Example:** Instead of saying, "I want to be fit," a SMART goal might be, "I will exercise for 30 minutes, five times a week for the next three months."

**Strategic Planning**
With your vision and goals in place, it's time to create a strategic plan. This plan outlines the steps you need to take to achieve your objectives and identifies the resources you will require.
Think of your strategic plan as a detailed map for your journey. It should include:

**Action steps**: Specific tasks you need to complete.

**Resources**: What tools, people, or materials you need.

**Timeline**: A schedule for when you will complete each step.

**Example:** If your goal is to launch a new product, your strategic plan might include steps like conducting market research, developing the product, and creating a marketing strategy.

## Execution and Adaptation

A well-laid plan is only as good as its execution. This is where many people stumble. Execution requires discipline, commitment, and the ability to stay focused on your goals.

Additionally, it is essential to remain adaptable. The landscape of our lives is constantly changing, and new challenges can arise at any moment. Regularly review your progress and be prepared to make adjustments to your strategy as needed.

**Example:** If your initial marketing plan for your product launch isn't generating interest, be willing to pivot and try new approaches rather than sticking rigidly to your original plan.

## Measuring Success

To know whether you are on track for strategic success, you must measure your progress. This involves establishing key performance indicators (KPIs) that help you assess whether you are meeting your goals.

KPIs can vary based on your objectives but can include metrics like revenue growth, customer satisfaction scores, or personal milestones like weight loss or skill development. Regularly review these indicators to gauge your progress and make informed decisions moving forward.

**Example:** If your goal is to increase sales by 20% in a year, track your monthly sales figures to see if you're on pace to reach that target.

# THE ROLE OF REFLECTION AND LEARNING

Strategic success is also about continuous improvement. Reflecting on your experiences—both successes and failures—provides valuable insights. What worked well? What could you have done differently? Embracing a growth mindset means viewing setbacks as learning opportunities rather than failures.

Take time to journal your reflections. Write down what you learn from each step of your journey, and use these insights to inform your future actions.

# CONCLUSION: YOUR JOURNEY BEGINS

Understanding strategic success is the first step on your path to achieving your goals. By developing a clear vision, setting meaningful objectives, creating a strategic plan, executing with discipline, and reflecting on your progress, you are laying the groundwork for a successful future.

As you move forward in this book, keep in mind that every journey is unique. Your experiences, challenges, and victories will shape your understanding of strategic success in ways that are distinctly yours. Embrace the journey, stay committed, and remember that strategic success is not just about the destination—it's about the growth and learning that happens along the way.

**Homework:**

Write a personal definition of strategic success. Reflect on what it means to you and how it aligns with your life goals.

Identify and draft a vision statement for your personal or professional life. Make it inspiring and clear, outlining where you want to be in the future.

As you work on these assignments, keep in mind that the foundation of strategic success begins with clarity and intention. You have the power to shape your future—let's start building it!

# CHAPTER 2: THE FOUNDATION OF STRATEGY

Every successful journey begins with a solid foundation, and when it comes to achieving strategic success, that foundation is strategy itself. Strategy serves as the blueprint for how you will achieve your goals and navigate the challenges that may arise along the way. In this chapter, we will explore the fundamental elements of strategy, including how to analyse your environment, set clear objectives, and build a robust foundation for your future endeavours.

# WHAT IS STRATEGY?

At its core, **strategy** is a plan of action designed to achieve specific goals. It is a systematic approach that enables you to make informed decisions and allocate resources effectively. Think of strategy as the roadmap for your journey; it outlines the best routes to take, potential detours, and alternative paths if obstacles arise.

While the term "strategy" is often associated with military operations or corporate business, it can be applied to various aspects of life, from personal goals to team projects. Regardless of the context, the principles of strategy remain consistent: clarity, foresight, and adaptability.

# THE IMPORTANCE OF STRATEGIC ANALYSIS

Before developing a strategy, it's crucial to analyse your current environment and understand the factors that may influence your success. This analysis involves examining both the internal and external factors affecting your situation.

**Internal Analysis**
Internal analysis focuses on understanding your strengths and weaknesses. What resources do you have at your disposal? What skills or talents do you possess? Reflecting on these questions can help you identify areas where you excel and areas that may require improvement.

Tools like the **SWOT analysis** (Strengths, Weaknesses, Opportunities, Threats) can be incredibly helpful in this phase. By assessing your internal strengths and weaknesses, you can better position yourself to capitalise on your advantages and address any shortcomings.

**Example:** If you're launching a new product, your internal analysis may reveal strengths such as a talented team, robust funding, and innovative technology. However, it may also expose weaknesses, such as limited marketing experience or a small customer base.

**External Analysis**
External analysis involves evaluating the broader environment in which you operate. This includes market trends, competitive forces, and socio-economic factors that may impact your

goals. Tools like **PESTEL analysis** (Political, Economic, Social, Technological, Environmental, and Legal) can help you identify these external factors.

Understanding the external landscape is essential for anticipating challenges and recognizing opportunities. For example, emerging technologies might present new avenues for growth, while economic downturns could necessitate a shift in strategy.

**Example:** In the case of your new product launch, external analysis might uncover a growing demand for eco-friendly products or increased competition from established brands. Recognizing these factors allows you to adapt your strategy accordingly.

# SETTING CLEAR OBJECTIVES

Once you have conducted a thorough analysis of your environment, the next step is to establish clear objectives. Objectives are specific, measurable outcomes that guide your actions and serve as benchmarks for success.

Here are some key aspects to consider when setting objectives:

**Alignment with Vision and Mission**
Ensure that your objectives align with your overarching vision and mission. This alignment creates a sense of coherence in your strategy, allowing you to stay focused on what truly matters.
**Example:** If your vision is to promote sustainable living, an objective could be to reduce your company's carbon footprint by 30% over the next five years.

**SMART Criteria**
To create effective objectives, apply the SMART criteria discussed in the previous chapter:

**Specific**: Clearly define what you want to achieve.

**Measurable**: Identify how you will track progress.

**Achievable**: Set realistic objectives based on your resources and capabilities.

**Relevant**: Ensure your objectives contribute to your overall vision and mission.

**Time-bound**: Establish deadlines for achieving your objectives.

**Example:** Instead of a vague objective like "improve customer satisfaction," a SMART objective might be "increase customer satisfaction ratings from 75% to 90% within one year."

# DEVELOPING A STRATEGIC PLAN

With a solid understanding of your environment and clear objectives in place, it's time to create a strategic plan. This plan will serve as your action blueprint, detailing the steps you will take to achieve your objectives.

## Action Steps

Break down your objectives into actionable steps. Each action should be specific and assigned to responsible individuals or teams. This clarity promotes accountability and ensures that everyone knows what is expected of them.

**Example:** If your objective is to increase sales by 20% within a year, action steps might include launching a new marketing campaign, enhancing your online presence, and training your sales team.

## Resource Allocation

Assess the resources you have available, including time, budget, personnel, and technology. Determine how you will allocate these resources effectively to support your strategic plan.

**Example:** If your marketing campaign requires additional funding, you may need to reallocate budget from another department or seek external financing.

## Timeline and Milestones

Create a timeline for your strategic plan, highlighting key milestones along the way. Milestones serve as checkpoints that allow you to monitor progress and make necessary adjustments.

**Example:** For your sales objective, milestones could include achieving a 5% increase in sales after three months, a 10% increase after six months, and so on.

# THE ROLE OF FLEXIBILITY AND ADAPTATION

Even with a well-laid plan, it's essential to remain flexible and ready to adapt. The business landscape is constantly evolving, and new challenges may arise unexpectedly. Regularly review your progress, assess the effectiveness of your strategy, and be willing to pivot when necessary.

**Feedback Loops**
Establish feedback loops to gather insights from your team and stakeholders. Encourage open communication and create an environment where feedback is valued. This practice fosters collaboration and enables you to identify potential issues early on.
**Example:** Hold regular team meetings to discuss progress, challenges, and opportunities for improvement. Use this input to refine your strategic plan.

**Continuous Learning**
Embrace a mindset of continuous learning. The world is full of new ideas and innovative approaches. Stay informed about industry trends, best practices, and emerging technologies that may enhance your strategy.
**Example:** Attend workshops, webinars, and conferences related to your field. Engage with thought leaders and seek opportunities to learn from others' experiences.

# CONCLUSION: BUILDING A STRONG FOUNDATION

In this chapter, we explored the foundational elements of strategy, including the importance of strategic analysis, the process of setting clear objectives, and the steps involved in developing a robust strategic plan. By establishing a solid foundation, you equip yourself with the tools needed to navigate the complexities of your journey toward strategic success.

As you move forward, remember that strategy is not static. It requires ongoing assessment, adaptation, and a commitment to learning. The world is constantly changing, and your ability to adapt your strategy accordingly will determine your success.

**Homework:**

Conduct a SWOT analysis of your current situation. Identify your strengths, weaknesses, opportunities, and threats, and reflect on how these factors influence your strategic planning.

Set at least two SMART objectives for your personal or professional life. Write them down and outline the specific actions you will take to achieve them.

By engaging in these exercises, you will deepen your understanding of the strategic foundation and gain practical insights that will serve you well in your journey toward success.

Let's continue building on this foundation as we explore how to cultivate a strategic mindset in the next chapter!

# CHAPTER 3: CULTIVATING A STRATEGIC MINDSET

As we dive into the concept of a strategic mindset, it's important to understand that having a strategic mindset is not just about thinking; it's about cultivating a way of approaching challenges and opportunities that enables you to make informed decisions and take calculated actions. This chapter will explore the elements that contribute to a strategic mindset and provide practical guidance on how to develop this crucial way of thinking.

# WHAT IS A STRATEGIC MINDSET?

A **strategic mindset** involves a mental framework that enables you to assess situations from multiple angles, anticipate potential outcomes, and make decisions that align with your long-term objectives. It is characterised by forward-thinking, adaptability, and a willingness to learn. When you cultivate a strategic mindset, you become better equipped to navigate complexities and uncertainties, ultimately enhancing your chances of success.

# THE COMPONENTS OF A STRATEGIC MINDSET

To effectively cultivate a strategic mindset, it's essential to understand its key components. Each element contributes to how you perceive challenges, evaluate options, and make decisions.

**Vision and Long-term Thinking**
Having a clear vision of what you want to achieve is foundational to a strategic mindset. This vision serves as your guiding star, helping you remain focused on your long-term goals. A visionary mindset encourages you to think beyond immediate tasks and consider the bigger picture.

**Example:** If you envision yourself as a leader in sustainable business practices, your decisions and actions will be geared toward building a brand that prioritises environmental responsibility, even if it requires short-term sacrifices.

**Critical Thinking and Analysis**
A strategic mindset involves critically analysing situations and data before making decisions. This means questioning assumptions, evaluating evidence, and considering various perspectives. Critical thinking allows you to separate emotion from logic and make decisions based on facts rather than impulses.

**Example:** Before launching a new product, conduct thorough market research to understand customer needs, analyse competitor offerings, and assess potential risks. This critical analysis will inform your strategy and enhance your chances of success.

**Adaptability and Resilience**

In a world that is constantly changing, adaptability is crucial. A strategic mindset embraces flexibility, allowing you to pivot your approach when faced with new information or unexpected challenges. Resilience is equally important; it empowers you to recover from setbacks and continue pursuing your goals with determination.

**Example:** If a marketing campaign does not yield the expected results, instead of becoming discouraged, assess the situation, learn from the experience, and adapt your strategy accordingly. This resilience ensures that you remain on track despite obstacles.

**Collaborative Thinking**

Strategic thinking is often enhanced through collaboration. Engaging with diverse perspectives fosters creativity and innovation. A collaborative mindset values input from others, recognizes the strengths of a team, and encourages collective problem-solving.

**Example:** In a brainstorming session, encourage team members to share their ideas without judgement. This open dialogue can lead to innovative solutions and a deeper understanding of the challenges at hand.

# DEVELOPING YOUR STRATEGIC MINDSET

Now that we've explored the components of a strategic mindset, let's discuss how to develop and cultivate this way of thinking in your own life.

**Set Clear Goals and Objectives**
Start by defining clear, specific, and achievable goals. Write them down and regularly review them to ensure that you stay aligned with your vision. Setting goals provides direction and helps you maintain focus on what truly matters.

**Practical Tip:** Use the SMART criteria (Specific, Measurable, Achievable, Relevant, Time-bound) when setting your goals. For instance, instead of saying, "I want to improve my career," set a goal like, "I want to earn a certification in my field within the next six months."

**Embrace Continuous Learning**
Cultivating a strategic mindset requires a commitment to lifelong learning. Stay curious, seek new knowledge, and be open to different perspectives. This continuous learning approach allows you to stay updated on industry trends, best practices, and emerging technologies.

**Practical Tip:** Dedicate time each week to read books, listen to podcasts, or attend workshops related to your field. Engage with thought leaders and experts to gain fresh insights and broaden your understanding.

## Practice Reflection and Self-Assessment

Regularly reflect on your decisions and actions. What worked well? What could have been done differently? Self-assessment promotes self-awareness and allows you to identify areas for improvement.

**Practical Tip:** After completing a project or achieving a goal, take time to evaluate the process. Write down your reflections and lessons learned, which can inform your future strategies.

## Cultivate a Problem-Solving Mindset

Develop a proactive approach to problem-solving. When faced with challenges, focus on identifying solutions rather than dwelling on obstacles. A problem-solving mindset encourages creativity and resourcefulness.

**Practical Tip:** When encountering a problem, brainstorm multiple solutions and evaluate their pros and cons. Choose the best course of action and be willing to adjust if necessary.

## Surround Yourself with Diverse Thinkers

Engage with individuals who possess diverse perspectives and backgrounds. Surrounding yourself with a variety of thinkers can enrich your understanding and challenge your assumptions.

**Practical Tip:** Join professional groups, forums, or networks where you can connect with people from different industries and backgrounds. Participate in discussions and embrace the opportunity to learn from others.

## Emphasise Emotional Intelligence

Developing emotional intelligence (EQ) enhances your ability to navigate complex social dynamics and make informed decisions. EQ involves understanding your emotions and the emotions of others, which is essential for effective communication and collaboration.

**Practical Tip:** Practise active listening when engaging with others. Acknowledge their feelings and perspectives, and respond thoughtfully. This practice builds rapport and fosters collaboration.

# OVERCOMING CHALLENGES TO DEVELOPING A STRATEGIC MINDSET

While cultivating a strategic mindset is essential, it's important to acknowledge the challenges that may arise. Here are some common obstacles and strategies to overcome them:

**Fear of Failure**
The fear of failure can paralyse decision-making and inhibit risk-taking. Recognize that failure is often a stepping stone to success. Embrace the idea that mistakes are valuable learning opportunities.

**Strategy:** Shift your perspective by reframing failure as a chance to grow. After a setback, ask yourself, "What can I learn from this experience?" This approach reduces fear and encourages a more resilient mindset.

**Limited Perspective**
Relying solely on your own experiences can create blind spots. To develop a strategic mindset, you must actively seek diverse viewpoints and challenge your assumptions.

**Strategy:** Engage in discussions with people from different backgrounds and industries. Actively seek feedback and be open to differing opinions. This exposure broadens your perspective and enhances your strategic thinking.

**Overwhelming Complexity**

The complexities of modern life can feel overwhelming, making it difficult to focus on strategic thinking. To combat this, break down challenges into manageable components.

**Strategy:** When faced with a complex problem, outline the key factors involved and prioritise them. Focus on addressing one aspect at a time, which will help reduce feelings of overwhelm.

# CONCLUSION: EMBRACING YOUR STRATEGIC JOURNEY

As we conclude this chapter on cultivating a strategic mindset, remember that developing this way of thinking is a journey, not a destination. It requires dedication, practice, and a willingness to learn from both successes and failures. By embracing the components of a strategic mindset and actively applying them in your life, you will position yourself for greater success and fulfilment.

Your strategic journey begins with the mindset you cultivate. As you move forward, take the time to reflect on your goals, embrace continuous learning, and foster collaboration with others. With a strategic mindset, you will navigate challenges with confidence and seize opportunities that lead you closer to your vision.

**Homework:**

Write down three long-term goals that align with your vision. For each goal, list the specific actions you will take to achieve them.

Identify a recent challenge you faced and reflect on how you approached it. What did you learn from the experience, and how can you apply that learning to future challenges?

By engaging in these exercises, you will reinforce your understanding of a strategic mindset and begin to implement these principles in your daily life. Let's continue our exploration in the next chapter as we delve into the strategic planning process!

# CHAPTER 4: CRAFTING A WINNING STRATEGY

In our journey toward strategic success, we arrive at a crucial juncture: crafting a winning strategy. This chapter delves into the art and science of developing a strategy that not only resonates with your vision but also guides your actions and decisions toward achieving your goals. Whether you're an entrepreneur launching a new venture, a leader in an organisation, or simply someone eager to make positive changes in your life, understanding how to create a winning strategy is essential.

# WHAT IS A WINNING STRATEGY?

A **winning strategy** is a well-defined plan that outlines how you will achieve your goals. It serves as a roadmap, guiding your actions and helping you make decisions aligned with your long-term vision. A strong strategy takes into account the current landscape, identifies opportunities and threats, and leverages your strengths to navigate challenges.

To put it simply, a winning strategy provides clarity. It clarifies where you are going, how you plan to get there, and what success looks like along the way.

# THE STRATEGIC PLANNING PROCESS

Creating a winning strategy is not a one-time event; it's an ongoing process that requires careful thought and consideration. The following steps outline a strategic planning process that can help you craft an effective strategy:

**Define Your Vision and Goals**
Before you can develop a strategy, it's essential to have a clear vision and specific goals. Your vision is your ultimate destination, while your goals are the milestones you'll reach along the way.

**Practical Tip:** Take time to write down your vision statement and list at least three specific goals that align with that vision. For example, if your vision is to become a leader in sustainable fashion, your goals could include launching an eco-friendly clothing line, establishing partnerships with sustainable suppliers, and increasing brand awareness by 30% within the next year.

**Conduct a SWOT Analysis**
A SWOT analysis is a powerful tool that helps you assess your strengths, weaknesses, opportunities, and threats. This analysis provides valuable insights into your current position and the external environment.

**Strengths:** What advantages do you have? These could include unique skills, resources, or experiences that set you apart from others.

**Weaknesses:** What areas need improvement? Identifying weaknesses allows you to address them and turn them into opportunities for growth.

**Opportunities:** What external factors could you leverage for success? These might include emerging trends, market gaps, or changes in consumer behaviour.

**Threats:** What challenges could hinder your progress? Recognizing potential threats enables you to develop strategies to mitigate them.

**Practical Tip:** Create a SWOT analysis chart on a piece of paper. Fill in each quadrant with relevant information and use this analysis to inform your strategy.

**Identify Key Strategies and Tactics**
Once you have a clear understanding of your strengths, weaknesses, opportunities, and threats, it's time to develop key strategies that will guide your actions. Strategies are high-level approaches to achieving your goals, while tactics are the specific actions you'll take to implement those strategies.

**Example:** If one of your goals is to increase brand awareness, a key strategy might be to enhance your online presence. Tactics could include launching a social media campaign, collaborating with influencers, and optimising your website for search engines.

**Practical Tip:** For each goal, outline at least two to three key strategies, and then break those down into actionable tactics. This will help you create a comprehensive plan that is easy to follow.

**Establish Metrics for Success**
To measure the effectiveness of your strategy, it's essential to establish clear metrics for success. Metrics provide tangible indicators of progress and help you determine whether you're on track to achieve your goals.

**Example:** If your goal is to increase sales by 20% over the next year, your metrics could include monthly sales figures, customer acquisition rates, and website traffic statistics.

**Practical Tip:** Write down specific metrics for each goal and set a timeline for tracking them. Regularly review these metrics to assess your progress and make adjustments as needed.

### Create an Action Plan

An action plan outlines the specific steps you will take to implement your strategy. It should include deadlines, responsibilities, and resources required to execute each tactic. A well-structured action plan keeps you organised and accountable.

**Practical Tip:** Use a project management tool or a simple spreadsheet to create your action plan. Include columns for tasks, responsible parties, deadlines, and status updates. This visual representation will help you stay focused and on track.

### Implement and Monitor Progress

With your strategy and action plan in place, it's time to implement your plan. As you execute your tactics, monitor your progress regularly. This includes reviewing your metrics, assessing the effectiveness of your strategies, and making necessary adjustments.

**Practical Tip:** Schedule regular check-ins (weekly or monthly) to evaluate your progress. This could involve reviewing your metrics, discussing challenges with your team (if applicable), and celebrating milestones.

### Adapt and Evolve

The business landscape is dynamic, and your strategy may need to evolve as circumstances change. Stay open to feedback and be willing to pivot your approach when necessary. Adaptability is key to long-term success.

**Practical Tip:** Encourage a culture of feedback among your team (if applicable) and remain receptive to new ideas and suggestions. Regularly reassess your SWOT analysis and adjust your strategy based on changing conditions.

# COMMON PITFALLS TO AVOID

While crafting a winning strategy is essential, there are common pitfalls that can derail your efforts. Here are some challenges to be mindful of:

**Lack of Clarity**
Without a clear vision and well-defined goals, your strategy may lack direction. Ensure that your vision statement is specific and resonates with your core values.

**Strategy:** Share your vision with trusted peers or mentors for feedback. This can help clarify your ideas and provide insights into how others perceive your goals.

**Ignoring the Competition**
Failing to analyse your competitors can result in missed opportunities. Understanding the competitive landscape allows you to differentiate yourself and identify gaps in the market.

**Strategy:** Conduct regular competitor analysis. This could involve reviewing their websites, social media, and marketing strategies. Use this information to refine your own approach.

**Neglecting Follow-Through**
A well-crafted strategy is only effective if it's implemented. Neglecting to follow through on your action plan can lead to stagnation and missed opportunities.

**Strategy:** Hold yourself accountable by setting regular check-ins and progress reviews. Consider partnering with an accountability buddy to keep each other on track.

**Overcomplicating the Strategy**

A complex strategy can be overwhelming and difficult to execute. Keep your strategy straightforward and focused on your key goals.

**Strategy:** Limit the number of goals and strategies you pursue at once. This allows you to concentrate your efforts and achieve more meaningful results.

# CONCLUSION: THE PATH TO STRATEGIC SUCCESS

Crafting a winning strategy is a vital step on your journey to strategic success. By defining your vision, conducting a SWOT analysis, identifying key strategies, and establishing metrics, you lay the groundwork for achieving your goals. Remember that a strategy is not a static document; it requires ongoing monitoring and adaptation to remain relevant in a changing environment.

As you move forward, embrace the mindset of continuous improvement. Seek feedback, celebrate your achievements, and be willing to adjust your approach as needed. The process of crafting and refining your strategy is just as important as the outcomes you achieve.

With a well-crafted strategy in hand, you are well-equipped to navigate challenges, seize opportunities, and move confidently toward your vision of success.

**Homework:**

Create your own SWOT analysis, focusing on your current situation, skills, and aspirations. Fill out each quadrant thoughtfully.

Develop a strategic plan for one specific goal you want to achieve in the next six months. Outline key strategies and actionable tactics, and establish metrics to track your progress.

By engaging in these exercises, you will gain practical experience in crafting a winning strategy, setting the stage for your continued growth and success. Let's explore the next chapter, where we'll discuss the art of effective execution!

# CHAPTER 5: EXECUTION: TURNING STRATEGY INTO ACTION

Crafting a winning strategy is only half the battle in the journey toward strategic success. The real challenge lies in execution—the process of turning your carefully devised plans into tangible actions. Execution is where the rubber meets the road, and without effective execution, even the most brilliant strategies can fall flat. In this chapter, we will explore the critical importance of execution, the challenges that can arise, and practical steps you can take to ensure that your strategies are successfully brought to life.

# THE IMPORTANCE OF EXECUTION

Execution is the bridge between strategy and results. It involves translating your strategic vision into real-world actions that drive progress toward your goals. Effective execution requires not just clarity in your strategy but also commitment, coordination, and communication among all stakeholders involved.

**Why Execution Matters**

**Realising Goals:** No matter how well-defined your goals are, they remain theoretical until you take action. Execution is the step that transforms ideas into reality.

**Building Momentum:** Successful execution generates momentum. Each small victory adds to your confidence and encourages further progress.

**Learning and Adapting:** The execution phase provides valuable insights. By implementing your strategy, you can identify what works, what doesn't, and where adjustments are needed.

**The Cost of Poor Execution**
Failing to execute effectively can lead to wasted resources, missed opportunities, and frustration. Here are some common consequences of poor execution:

**Stagnation:** When strategies are not put into action, organisations can become stagnant, falling behind competitors who are willing to take risks and innovate.

**Loss of Trust:** Stakeholders—whether they are employees, customers, or investors—can lose trust if they perceive that the organisation is not following through on its commitments.

**Increased Stress:** The longer a strategy remains unexecuted, the greater the pressure builds. This can lead to stress and burnout among team members.

# COMMON CHALLENGES IN EXECUTION

While execution is vital, it is also fraught with challenges. Understanding these challenges can help you navigate them effectively:

**Lack of Clarity**
A lack of clarity in roles, responsibilities, and objectives can hinder execution. If team members are uncertain about what is expected of them, progress will stall.

**Solution:** Clearly define roles and responsibilities for each team member. Use a project management tool to outline tasks and deadlines, ensuring everyone knows their contributions.

**Poor Communication**
Effective communication is essential for successful execution. Miscommunication can lead to misunderstandings, wasted time, and conflicts.

**Solution:** Establish regular communication channels, such as team meetings or check-ins, to ensure everyone is aligned and informed. Utilise collaborative tools to facilitate transparent communication.

**Inadequate Resources**
Insufficient resources—be it time, budget, or personnel—can

impede execution. Without the necessary support, even the best strategies can falter.

**Solution:** Assess your resource needs during the planning phase. Ensure you have a realistic budget and allocate sufficient time for each task. If necessary, consider delegating tasks or bringing in additional support.

**Resistance to Change**

People are often resistant to change, especially if they are accustomed to established processes. This resistance can slow down execution.

**Solution:** Foster a culture of openness and adaptability. Engage team members in discussions about the changes and emphasise the benefits of the new strategies. Provide training if necessary to ease the transition.

**Overcomplication**

Strategies that are too complex can lead to confusion and paralysis. When team members are overwhelmed, they may struggle to take action.

**Solution:** Simplify your action plans. Focus on the most critical tasks that will drive progress toward your goals. Break down large tasks into manageable steps.

# STEPS TO EFFECTIVE EXECUTION

Now that we've addressed the importance of execution and the common challenges, let's discuss practical steps you can take to turn strategy into action:

**Create an Action Plan**
An action plan is a detailed document that outlines the specific steps you will take to implement your strategy. It should include timelines, responsibilities, and resources needed.

**Practical Tip:** Use a project management tool or a simple spreadsheet to create your action plan. Include columns for tasks, responsible parties, deadlines, and status updates. This visual representation will help you stay organised.

**Set Clear Milestones**
Milestones are significant points along your journey that indicate progress. They serve as checkpoints to evaluate whether you are on track.

**Practical Tip:** Break down your goals into smaller, achievable milestones. For instance, if your goal is to launch a new product in six months, establish milestones for market research, product development, and marketing strategies.

**Allocate Resources Wisely**
Ensure that you have the necessary resources—both human and financial—to support your execution efforts. Assign team members based on their strengths and expertise.

**Practical Tip:** Conduct a resource audit before starting your action plan. Identify any gaps in your team's skill sets or budgetary constraints and make adjustments as needed.

### Implement Accountability Mechanisms

Accountability is crucial for successful execution. Establish systems that hold team members accountable for their contributions to the project.

**Practical Tip:** Use regular check-ins to discuss progress and challenges. Consider implementing a system of peer reviews or project updates to encourage accountability and collaboration.

### Monitor Progress and Adapt

As you implement your action plan, regularly monitor your progress against the established milestones and metrics. Be open to feedback and willing to adapt your approach if necessary.

**Practical Tip:** Schedule regular evaluation sessions (weekly or monthly) to assess progress. Review your metrics, celebrate successes, and address any roadblocks.

### Celebrate Small Wins

Celebrating small wins is essential for maintaining motivation and momentum. Recognizing progress boosts team morale and reinforces the value of effective execution.

**Practical Tip:** Create a culture of celebration by acknowledging achievements, both big and small. Consider hosting team lunches or shout-outs during meetings to highlight progress.

# CASE STUDIES OF EFFECTIVE EXECUTION

**Apple Inc. – Launching the iPhone**
Apple's launch of the iPhone is a prime example of successful execution. The company had a clear vision and meticulously planned every aspect of the product launch, from marketing to supply chain management. Apple's commitment to quality and attention to detail allowed them to execute their strategy flawlessly, leading to a product that revolutionised the smartphone industry.

**Starbucks – Global Expansion**
Starbucks is another company that has effectively executed its strategic vision. The company focused on creating a unique customer experience, emphasising quality and community. By consistently monitoring customer feedback and adapting to local markets, Starbucks has successfully expanded its presence globally while maintaining its brand identity.

**Amazon – Continuous Improvement**
Amazon's commitment to execution is evident in its focus on continuous improvement. The company regularly analyses customer data to refine its offerings and streamline operations. This dedication to execution has enabled Amazon to dominate the e-commerce market and continually innovate its services.

# CONCLUSION: BRIDGING STRATEGY AND SUCCESS

Effective execution is the cornerstone of turning strategy into action. By creating a clear action plan, setting milestones, allocating resources wisely, and fostering a culture of accountability, you position yourself for success. Remember that execution is not a one-time event but an ongoing process that requires commitment, adaptability, and continuous improvement.

As you implement your strategies, embrace the journey. Celebrate your progress, learn from your experiences, and remain open to adjustments. With a solid execution plan in place, you can confidently navigate the challenges and uncertainties that come your way, ultimately leading to strategic success.

**Homework:**

Create a detailed action plan for one of your strategic goals, including specific tasks, responsible individuals, deadlines, and necessary resources.

Identify at least three milestones for your goal and outline metrics to track progress. Schedule regular check-ins to review your progress and make adjustments as needed.

By engaging in these exercises, you'll develop a deeper

understanding of execution and its critical role in achieving your strategic goals. In the next chapter, we'll explore the art of measuring and evaluating success, ensuring that your efforts lead to meaningful outcomes.

# CHAPTER 6: MEASURING SUCCESS AND ADAPTING

As you embark on your journey toward strategic success, one critical component cannot be overlooked: measurement. Understanding how to measure success and being willing to adapt are vital skills that will not only guide your progress but also enhance your ability to make informed decisions. In this chapter, we will explore the importance of measuring success, various metrics you can use, and how to adapt your strategies based on what you learn.

# THE IMPORTANCE OF MEASURING SUCCESS

Measuring success is essential for several reasons:

**Evaluating Progress**
Tracking your progress helps you understand where you stand in relation to your goals. Are you on track, ahead, or behind schedule? Measuring success gives you a clear picture of your achievements and areas that require attention.

**Informing Decision-Making**
Data-driven decision-making is far more effective than relying solely on intuition. By measuring success, you can gather valuable insights that help you make informed choices about future strategies, resource allocation, and adjustments.

**Accountability**
Establishing metrics creates accountability within your team. When everyone understands what success looks like and how it will be measured, they are more likely to stay focused and committed to achieving those objectives.

**Continuous Improvement**
Measurement fosters a culture of continuous improvement. By regularly assessing performance, you can identify strengths and weaknesses, making it easier to refine processes and enhance outcomes.

# KEY METRICS FOR MEASURING SUCCESS

To effectively measure success, it's essential to select the right metrics that align with your goals. Here are some common metrics across various domains:

**Key Performance Indicators (KPIs)**
KPIs are quantifiable metrics that reflect the critical success factors of an organisation. They provide a snapshot of performance and progress toward strategic objectives. Examples of KPIs include:

**Sales Revenue:** A clear indicator of financial performance and growth.

**Customer Satisfaction Scores:** Reflects how well you are meeting customer expectations.

**Employee Engagement Levels:** Indicates how motivated and committed your employees are.

**Return on Investment (ROI)**
ROI measures the profitability of an investment relative to its cost. It's a valuable metric for evaluating the effectiveness of marketing campaigns, projects, or new initiatives.

**Calculation:** ROI = (Net Profit / Cost of Investment) x 100

**Market Share**
Market share is the percentage of an industry or market's total sales that is earned by a particular company. Tracking your

market share helps you understand your position relative to competitors.

**Customer Acquisition Cost (CAC)**
CAC measures the cost of acquiring a new customer. Understanding this metric helps you evaluate the effectiveness of your marketing strategies and adjust your budget accordingly.

**Calculation:** CAC = Total Sales and Marketing Expenses / Number of New Customers Acquired

**Net Promoter Score (NPS)**
NPS measures customer loyalty and satisfaction by asking customers how likely they are to recommend your product or service to others. It's a simple yet powerful tool for gauging customer sentiment.

**Time to Market**
This metric tracks the time it takes to develop and launch a new product or service. Reducing time to market can give you a competitive edge, so it's essential to monitor and improve this process.

**Employee Turnover Rate**
A high turnover rate can indicate issues within your organisation, such as low morale or inadequate management. Monitoring this metric helps you identify areas for improvement within your workplace culture.

# GATHERING AND ANALYSING DATA

Once you've selected your metrics, the next step is to gather and analyse data. Here's how you can effectively collect and interpret the information:

**Utilise Data Collection Tools**
Modern technology offers numerous tools for data collection and analysis. Consider using software platforms like Google Analytics, CRM systems, or project management tools that provide insights into performance metrics.

**Set Up Regular Reporting**
Establish a routine for reporting on your metrics. Whether weekly, monthly, or quarterly, regular reporting ensures you stay informed about your progress and can make timely adjustments.

**Visualise Data**
Data visualisation tools, such as charts and graphs, can help make complex data easier to understand. Visual representations allow you to quickly identify trends, patterns, and outliers.

**Engage Your Team**
Involve your team in the data collection process. Encourage them to share insights and interpretations of the data. This collaborative approach fosters a sense of ownership and commitment to the measurement process.

# ADAPTING BASED ON INSIGHTS

Collecting data is just the beginning; the real value comes from using that data to adapt your strategies. Here's how to effectively adapt based on your insights:

**Identify Trends and Patterns**
As you analyse your data, look for trends and patterns that emerge over time. Are there consistent areas of success? Are there recurring challenges? Understanding these patterns will inform your decisions moving forward.

**Be Open to Change**
Flexibility is essential for adaptation. If your metrics indicate that a strategy is not yielding the desired results, be willing to pivot. Embrace change as an opportunity for growth rather than a setback.

**Test and Iterate**
Implement changes incrementally and monitor their impact. Use A/B testing to compare different approaches and determine which one yields the best results. This iterative process helps you refine your strategies over time.

**Seek Feedback**
Gathering feedback from team members, customers, and stakeholders can provide valuable insights into how your strategies are perceived. Encourage open communication and be receptive to constructive criticism.

**Celebrate Successes**

When your adaptations lead to positive outcomes, celebrate those successes! Recognizing achievements fosters a culture of continuous improvement and motivates your team to keep pushing forward.

# CASE STUDIES: ADAPTING FOR SUCCESS

**Netflix – Evolving Content Strategy**
Netflix is a prime example of a company that continuously adapts its strategy based on data. Initially, the company focused on DVD rentals but quickly shifted to streaming as consumer preferences changed. By analysing viewer data, Netflix has refined its content offerings, leading to the production of popular original series and films.

**Zara – Fast Fashion and Responsiveness**
Zara, the fashion retailer, is known for its ability to quickly respond to changing fashion trends. The company measures sales data and customer feedback to adapt its inventory and design processes. This adaptability allows Zara to stay ahead of competitors and consistently meet customer demands.

**Procter & Gamble – Customer-Centric Innovation**
Procter & Gamble regularly engages with customers to gather feedback on its products. This customer-centric approach enables the company to adapt its product offerings based on real-world insights, leading to successful innovations and increased customer satisfaction.

# CONCLUSION: THE CYCLE OF MEASUREMENT AND ADAPTATION

Measuring success and adapting based on insights is a continuous cycle that drives strategic success. By establishing clear metrics, gathering and analysing data, and being willing to adapt, you position yourself for ongoing growth and improvement. Remember, the business landscape is dynamic, and your ability to respond to changing conditions will be a critical factor in achieving your strategic goals.

**Homework:**

Identify three key metrics relevant to your strategic goals. Create a plan for how you will gather and analyse data related to these metrics.

Choose one area of your strategy that has not been yielding the desired results. Develop a plan for how you will adapt your approach based on the insights you gather.

By engaging in these exercises, you will deepen your understanding of measurement and adaptation and enhance your ability to achieve strategic success. In the next chapter, we will explore the art of building resilience and maintaining focus on your long-term vision.

# CHAPTER 7: BUILDING A STRATEGIC TEAM

In any journey toward strategic success, one of the most critical components is your team. A well-structured and cohesive team can propel your strategic initiatives forward, while a disjointed or uninspired team can hinder progress. In this chapter, we'll explore the key elements of building a strategic team, including understanding team dynamics, fostering collaboration, identifying the right talent, and cultivating a culture of trust and accountability.

# UNDERSTANDING TEAM DYNAMICS

Before you can build an effective strategic team, it's essential to understand team dynamics—the interactions and relationships between team members. Recognizing how these dynamics impact your team's performance is crucial for success.

**Roles and Responsibilities**
Clearly defining roles and responsibilities is the first step in establishing a strong team dynamic. Each team member should understand their specific duties and how their contributions fit into the broader strategic objectives. When everyone knows their role, it reduces confusion and enhances accountability.

**Example:** In a marketing team, one member might focus on social media strategy, another on content creation, and yet another on data analysis. Each member should know how their work contributes to the overall marketing campaign.

**Complementary Skills**
A successful team consists of individuals with diverse skills and backgrounds. When team members bring different perspectives and expertise, they can approach challenges creatively and develop more comprehensive solutions.

**Tip:** During the hiring process, look for candidates who not only possess the necessary skills but also complement the existing team dynamics. Diversity in skill sets can lead to innovative thinking.

### Effective Communication

Open and honest communication is the lifeblood of any strategic team. Encourage team members to express their ideas, share feedback, and discuss challenges openly. Regular communication fosters collaboration and ensures that everyone is aligned toward common goals.

**Tools:** Consider using collaboration tools like Slack or Microsoft Teams to facilitate communication, especially if your team is working remotely or across different locations.

# FOSTERING COLLABORATION

Collaboration is a cornerstone of successful teamwork. When team members collaborate effectively, they can leverage each other's strengths and work together to achieve shared objectives.

**Creating a Collaborative Environment**
Establish an environment that encourages collaboration. This means breaking down silos and promoting cross-functional teamwork. Encourage team members from different departments to work together on projects or initiatives.

**Strategy:** Organise regular team-building activities that foster relationship-building and trust among team members. These activities can range from workshops to informal social gatherings.

**Setting Clear Goals**
Collaborating without clear goals can lead to confusion and frustration. Set specific, measurable, achievable, relevant, and time-bound (SMART) goals for your team. This clarity ensures that everyone is working toward the same objectives and allows for better coordination.

**Example:** Instead of setting a vague goal like "increase sales," a SMART goal would be "increase sales by 20% over the next quarter by launching two new marketing campaigns."

**Encouraging Idea Sharing**
Encourage team members to share their ideas and insights openly.

Create platforms, such as brainstorming sessions or idea boards, where everyone can contribute their thoughts. When team members feel their opinions are valued, they are more likely to engage in collaborative efforts.

# IDENTIFYING THE RIGHT TALENT

Building a strategic team requires careful consideration of the talent you bring on board. It's not just about hiring individuals with the right skills; it's also about finding people who align with your organisation's values and vision.

**Defining Your Ideal Team Member**
Before you start the hiring process, define the characteristics of your ideal team member. Consider qualities such as adaptability, problem-solving abilities, and a growth mindset. These traits are crucial for thriving in a dynamic strategic environment.

**Leveraging Networks and Referrals**
Often, the best candidates come from referrals. Encourage your current team members to recommend potential candidates they believe would fit well within the team. This approach not only saves time but also increases the likelihood of finding individuals who align with your team culture.

**Utilising Assessments and Interviews**
Use assessments and behavioural interviews to gauge candidates' compatibility with your team. These tools can help you identify how well candidates might work with others and whether they possess the necessary skills to contribute effectively to your strategy.

**Prioritising Cultural Fit**
Beyond skills and experience, assess how well candidates fit into

your organisational culture. A candidate who shares your values and vision is more likely to thrive and contribute positively to the team.

**Tip:** During interviews, ask questions that reveal a candidate's values, work style, and approach to teamwork. This insight can help you assess their cultural fit.

# CULTIVATING A CULTURE OF TRUST AND ACCOUNTABILITY

A strong team is built on trust and accountability. When team members trust each other, they are more likely to collaborate effectively and take ownership of their work.

**Establishing Trust**
Trust is cultivated through open communication, honesty, and reliability. Lead by example and demonstrate transparency in your actions and decisions. Encourage team members to do the same.

**Strategy:** Regularly hold team check-ins where members can discuss challenges, share progress, and offer support. This fosters a sense of camaraderie and builds trust within the team.

**Encouraging Accountability**
Accountability is about taking ownership of one's actions and outcomes. Create a culture where team members feel responsible for their contributions and outcomes. When individuals take pride in their work, they are more likely to strive for excellence.

**Tip:** Establish regular performance reviews where team members can reflect on their achievements and areas for improvement. This practice encourages accountability and promotes continuous growth.

**Recognizing Contributions**

Acknowledging and celebrating team members' contributions fosters a positive team environment. Recognize individual and team achievements publicly, whether through team meetings, emails, or company-wide announcements. Celebrating success boosts morale and motivates team members to continue striving for excellence.

**Example:** Implement a "team member of the month" program to highlight exceptional contributions and create a sense of recognition within the team.

# CONTINUOUS DEVELOPMENT AND TRAINING

To maintain a strategic edge, it's essential to invest in the continuous development of your team. As the business landscape evolves, so should your team's skills and knowledge.

**Providing Learning Opportunities**
Encourage team members to pursue professional development through workshops, conferences, or online courses. Investing in their growth not only enhances their skills but also demonstrates your commitment to their success.

**Strategy:** Set aside a budget for team training and development activities. This investment will pay off in increased productivity and employee satisfaction.

**Encouraging Knowledge Sharing**
Create a culture where team members share knowledge and expertise. Encourage them to conduct presentations or share insights from conferences or training sessions. Knowledge sharing enhances the collective intelligence of the team.

**Conducting Regular Feedback Sessions**
Implement regular feedback sessions to facilitate open dialogue between team members and leadership. Constructive feedback helps individuals identify areas for improvement and encourages continuous growth.

**Example:** Use 360-degree feedback methods where team members provide feedback to one another, creating a comprehensive view of performance and areas for development.

# CONCLUSION: THE POWER OF A STRATEGIC TEAM

Building a strategic team is a deliberate and ongoing process. By understanding team dynamics, fostering collaboration, identifying the right talent, cultivating a culture of trust and accountability, and investing in continuous development, you can create a powerhouse team capable of driving your strategic initiatives forward.

As you move forward, remember that a strong team is more than just a group of individuals; it's a cohesive unit that works together toward common goals. By prioritising teamwork and collaboration, you lay the foundation for strategic success that can adapt to challenges and seize opportunities.

**Homework:**

Reflect on your current team dynamics. Identify one area where communication can improve and develop a plan to enhance it.

Create a list of qualities you consider essential for a strategic team member. Use this list to assess future hires or to evaluate your current team's strengths and weaknesses.

By actively engaging with these exercises, you will deepen your understanding of the importance of building a strategic team and enhance your leadership skills. In the next chapter, we will explore the art of risk management and decision-making within your strategic journey.

# CHAPTER 8: NAVIGATING CHALLENGES AND OBSTACLES

In the journey toward strategic success, challenges and obstacles are inevitable. Whether you are an entrepreneur launching a new business, a manager overseeing a project, or a team leader guiding your group toward a common goal, you will encounter hurdles along the way. How you navigate these challenges can make a significant difference in your overall success. In this chapter, we will delve into the common challenges organisations face, explore effective strategies for overcoming them, and provide insights on maintaining resilience during tough times.

# UNDERSTANDING COMMON CHALLENGES

To effectively navigate challenges, it's essential first to identify what they are. Challenges can come in various forms, including:

**Market Changes**
The business landscape is constantly evolving. Changes in market demand, competition, and technological advancements can disrupt even the most well-laid strategic plans. Adapting to these changes is crucial for sustaining growth.

**Example:** Consider a retail company that relies heavily on in-store sales. If consumer behaviour shifts toward online shopping, the company must quickly adapt its strategy to remain competitive.

**Resource Constraints**
Limited resources, whether financial, human, or technological, can hinder progress. Many organisations struggle with balancing budgets, finding skilled employees, or investing in the latest technology.

**Tip:** Conduct a resource assessment to identify your organisation's strengths and weaknesses. This evaluation will help you allocate resources more effectively.

**Internal Resistance**
Change can be challenging, and resistance from team members is

a common obstacle. Employees may be hesitant to embrace new processes or strategies, leading to delays and decreased morale.

**Strategy:** Communicate the reasons for change clearly and involve team members in the decision-making process. When individuals feel included, they are more likely to support new initiatives.

### Unforeseen Circumstances

Life is unpredictable, and unforeseen circumstances such as economic downturns, natural disasters, or health crises can disrupt operations. Organisations must be prepared to pivot quickly in response to unexpected events.

**Example:** The COVID-19 pandemic forced many businesses to shift to remote work and adapt their strategies to accommodate new realities.

# STRATEGIES FOR OVERCOMING CHALLENGES

Now that we understand the common challenges, let's explore effective strategies for overcoming them:

**Fostering a Flexible Mindset**
A flexible mindset is essential for navigating challenges. Encourage your team to adopt a growth mindset, where they view obstacles as opportunities for learning and development. This perspective fosters resilience and adaptability.

**Tip:** Share stories of individuals or organisations that overcame challenges and emerged stronger. This can inspire your team and reinforce the idea that challenges are part of the journey.

**Implementing Agile Practices**
Agile practices promote adaptability and quick decision-making. By breaking projects into smaller, manageable tasks and iterating based on feedback, teams can respond more effectively to challenges.

**Example:** In software development, Agile methodologies allow teams to release products in stages, enabling them to incorporate user feedback and make adjustments in real-time.

**Building a Support Network**
Surround yourself with a supportive network of colleagues,

mentors, and industry peers. This network can provide valuable insights, advice, and encouragement when facing challenges.

**Strategy:** Attend industry conferences, join professional organisations, or participate in networking events to expand your connections and build relationships.

### Embracing Technology

Technology can be a powerful ally in overcoming challenges. Leverage tools and software that streamline processes, enhance communication, and improve efficiency. Investing in technology can help your organisation stay competitive and agile.

**Example:** Project management software like Trello or Asana can help teams track progress, assign tasks, and collaborate effectively, ensuring that everyone is aligned despite any challenges that arise.

# MAINTAINING RESILIENCE

Resilience is the ability to bounce back from setbacks and continue moving forward. Here are some strategies to help you and your team maintain resilience in the face of challenges:

**Cultivating a Positive Culture**
A positive organisational culture promotes resilience. Encourage an environment where team members feel safe to express their thoughts, share their concerns, and support one another.

**Tip:** Celebrate small wins and acknowledge team members' efforts, even in challenging times. Recognition boosts morale and fosters a sense of unity.

**Encouraging Open Communication**
Open lines of communication are vital during challenging times. Encourage team members to share their concerns, ideas, and feedback. By fostering a culture of transparency, you create an environment where individuals feel comfortable discussing challenges.

**Strategy:** Hold regular team meetings or check-ins to provide updates, discuss ongoing challenges, and solicit feedback from team members.

**Prioritising Well-Being**
The well-being of your team members is essential for resilience. Encourage work-life balance, provide resources for mental health, and promote self-care practices. When individuals feel supported,

they are better equipped to handle challenges.

**Example:** Offer flexible work arrangements, access to counselling services, or wellness programs to support your team's overall well-being.

**Learning from Failures**

Failures are valuable learning experiences. Instead of viewing setbacks as disasters, treat them as opportunities for growth. Analyse what went wrong, identify lessons learned, and apply those insights to future endeavours.

**Tip:** After a significant challenge or failure, conduct a debriefing session with your team to discuss what happened, what could have been done differently, and how to avoid similar issues in the future.

# EMBRACING CHANGE AS AN OPPORTUNITY

Change often brings uncertainty, but it also presents opportunities for growth and innovation. By embracing change rather than resisting it, you position yourself and your team to capitalise on new possibilities.

**Identifying Opportunities in Challenges**
When faced with a challenge, take a step back and assess the situation. Are there opportunities hidden within the obstacle? Perhaps a market shift presents a chance to innovate or create a new product line.

**Example:** During economic downturns, some businesses pivot to offer cost-effective solutions, attracting new customers and finding success in challenging times.

**Encouraging Innovation**
Encourage your team to think creatively when navigating challenges. Foster an environment where brainstorming and innovation are welcomed. New ideas often emerge when people are challenged to think outside the box.

**Strategy:** Set aside time for brainstorming sessions where team members can pitch innovative ideas and explore alternative approaches to overcoming obstacles.

**Being Proactive Rather than Reactive**
Rather than waiting for challenges to arise, take a proactive approach to anticipate potential obstacles. Conduct regular risk

assessments to identify vulnerabilities and develop contingency plans.

**Example:** If your organisation relies on a single supplier, consider diversifying your supply chain to mitigate risks associated with potential disruptions.

# CONCLUSION: A JOURNEY OF RESILIENCE AND GROWTH

Navigating challenges and obstacles is an integral part of the strategic success journey. By understanding common challenges, implementing effective strategies, and fostering resilience, you can empower yourself and your team to overcome hurdles and thrive.

Remember that challenges are not roadblocks; they are opportunities for growth and learning. Embrace the journey, and approach obstacles with a mindset of curiosity and determination. As you develop the skills to navigate challenges effectively, you will not only enhance your strategic abilities but also build a more resilient and adaptive organisation.

**Homework:**

Reflect on a recent challenge you faced in your personal or professional life. Write down the lessons learned and how you would approach a similar challenge differently in the future.

Identify three potential challenges your team might face in the coming months. Develop a proactive plan to address each challenge and share it with your team for feedback.

By engaging in these exercises, you will deepen your understanding of how to navigate challenges and obstacles, ultimately positioning yourself for greater strategic success. In the next chapter, we will explore the importance of continuous improvement and innovation in maintaining your strategic advantage.

# CHAPTER 9: FUTURE TRENDS IN STRATEGIC SUCCESS

As we navigate the complex and ever-changing landscape of business, understanding future trends in strategic success becomes essential. The world is evolving at an unprecedented pace, driven by advancements in technology, shifts in consumer behaviour, and changes in the global economy. In this chapter, we will explore emerging trends that are shaping strategic success and how organisations can adapt to thrive in the future.

# THE IMPACT OF TECHNOLOGY ON STRATEGY

One of the most significant influences on strategic success in the coming years will be technology. Rapid technological advancements are transforming the way businesses operate, communicate, and engage with customers. Here are some key areas where technology is making a profound impact:

**Artificial Intelligence (AI) and Automation**
AI is no longer a futuristic concept; it is actively reshaping industries today. Businesses are leveraging AI for various applications, from customer service chatbots to predictive analytics that help inform decision-making. Automation is also streamlining processes, allowing organisations to operate more efficiently.

**Adapting Strategy:** To stay competitive, organisations must embrace AI and automation in their strategies. This means investing in technology, training employees on new systems, and continuously evaluating how these tools can enhance productivity and customer engagement.

**Data-Driven Decision Making**
In the era of big data, organisations have access to vast amounts of information that can inform strategic decisions. Data analytics enables businesses to identify trends, understand customer

preferences, and measure the effectiveness of their strategies.

**Adapting Strategy:** Organisations must cultivate a data-driven culture. This involves investing in analytics tools, training employees to interpret data effectively, and using insights to guide strategic planning. The ability to make informed decisions based on data will be a critical factor in achieving success.

**Remote Work and Virtual Collaboration**
The COVID-19 pandemic accelerated the shift toward remote work, changing how organisations operate. Many companies have realised the benefits of flexibility, leading to a more permanent embrace of remote and hybrid work models.

**Adapting Strategy:** Embrace technology that facilitates virtual collaboration. Invest in communication tools and project management software to ensure teams can work together seamlessly, regardless of their physical location. Additionally, consider how remote work can influence talent acquisition, as it allows organisations to tap into a broader pool of candidates.

# SHIFTS IN CONSUMER BEHAVIOR

Understanding consumer behaviour is crucial for any organisation seeking strategic success. As societal values evolve, so do consumer expectations. Here are some trends that are reshaping how businesses engage with their customers:

**Increased Demand for Personalization**
Consumers today expect personalised experiences. From tailored product recommendations to customised marketing messages, individuals want brands to understand their unique needs and preferences.

**Adapting Strategy:** Use data and AI to create personalised experiences for customers. Implement customer relationship management (CRM) systems that track interactions and preferences, enabling you to deliver targeted marketing and recommendations that resonate with your audience.

**Focus on Sustainability and Social Responsibility**
As awareness of environmental and social issues grows, consumers are increasingly making purchasing decisions based on a brand's sustainability practices and social responsibility. They prefer to support companies that align with their values.

**Adapting Strategy:** Integrate sustainability into your business model. This may involve reducing waste, sourcing materials responsibly, or supporting local communities. Transparency about your practices can build trust and loyalty among consumers who prioritise ethical brands.

**Shift Toward Experiential Marketing**

Today's consumers value experiences over material possessions. They seek out brands that offer memorable interactions, whether through immersive events, engaging social media content, or interactive marketing campaigns.

**Adapting Strategy:** Invest in experiential marketing strategies that foster connections with your audience. Create memorable experiences that engage customers emotionally and encourage them to share their experiences with others.

# THE IMPORTANCE OF AGILITY AND ADAPTABILITY

In a world characterised by rapid change, agility and adaptability are no longer optional; they are essential for survival. Organisations must be willing to pivot their strategies in response to emerging trends and challenges.

**Embracing a Culture of Innovation**
Encouraging a culture of innovation within your organisation fosters agility. Empower employees to think creatively, experiment with new ideas, and challenge the status quo. This mindset will enable your organisation to respond quickly to market changes and seize opportunities.

**Adapting Strategy:** Allocate resources for research and development. Establish cross-functional teams that collaborate on innovative projects and encourage a safe environment for experimentation, where failures are viewed as opportunities for learning.

**Implementing Agile Methodologies**
Adopting agile methodologies allows organisations to respond quickly to changing circumstances. Agile practices, commonly used in software development, emphasise flexibility, collaboration, and iterative progress.

**Adapting Strategy:** Consider implementing agile project

management techniques within your organisation. Break projects into smaller tasks, prioritise work based on value, and regularly assess progress. This iterative approach allows for quick adjustments and fosters a sense of ownership among team members.

**Continuous Learning and Development**
The landscape of business is constantly evolving, making continuous learning essential. Organisations must prioritise professional development to keep employees equipped with the skills needed for future success.

**Adapting Strategy:** Offer ongoing training and development opportunities. This may include workshops, online courses, or mentorship programs that encourage employees to enhance their skills and stay current with industry trends.

# THE ROLE OF COLLABORATION AND NETWORKING

In an interconnected world, collaboration and networking will play a vital role in strategic success. Building relationships with other organisations, industry experts, and stakeholders can create synergies that drive innovation and growth.

**Strategic Partnerships**
Collaborating with other businesses can unlock new opportunities and resources. Strategic partnerships allow organisations to leverage each other's strengths, share knowledge, and access new markets.

**Adapting Strategy:** Identify potential partners that align with your goals and values. Explore opportunities for collaboration, whether through joint ventures, co-marketing initiatives, or shared resources.

**Networking and Community Engagement**
Engaging with industry networks and local communities can provide valuable insights and support. Building relationships with peers and stakeholders can enhance your organisation's reputation and foster collaboration.

**Adapting Strategy:** Attend industry events, join professional associations, and participate in community initiatives. Networking can open doors to new opportunities, partnerships, and insights that inform your strategic direction.

# PREPARING FOR THE FUTURE

As we look ahead to the future of strategic success, organisations must be proactive in adapting to changing landscapes. Here are some key takeaways to prepare for what lies ahead:

**Stay Informed About Trends**
Regularly monitor industry trends, consumer behaviour, and technological advancements. Subscribing to industry publications, following thought leaders on social media, and attending conferences can help you stay informed.

**Tip:** Set aside time each week to read articles, research reports, or listen to podcasts related to your industry. Staying informed will empower you to anticipate changes and adjust your strategies accordingly.

**Foster a Culture of Agility**
Encourage agility within your organisation by embracing change and fostering a culture that values adaptability. Empower employees to think creatively and make decisions that align with the organisation's goals.

**Tip:** Recognize and reward individuals and teams that demonstrate agility and innovation. Celebrating successes reinforces the importance of adaptability in achieving strategic success.

**Invest in Technology and Training**
Invest in technology that enhances collaboration, productivity,

and data-driven decision-making. Provide ongoing training and development opportunities to equip employees with the skills needed for success in a rapidly changing environment.

**Tip:** Consider conducting regular skills assessments to identify areas where additional training is needed. Tailor training programs to meet the specific needs of your team.

**Embrace a Long-Term Vision**

While it's essential to respond to immediate challenges, organisations must also maintain a long-term vision. Setting clear goals and objectives will guide decision-making and keep the organisation focused on strategic success.

**Tip:** Develop a strategic roadmap that outlines your organisation's goals for the next five to ten years. Regularly review and adjust this roadmap to reflect changes in the market and internal priorities.

# CONCLUSION: THE FUTURE AWAITS

In conclusion, the future of strategic success is filled with both challenges and opportunities. By understanding emerging trends, embracing technology, fostering agility, and building meaningful relationships, organisations can position themselves for success in an ever-evolving landscape.

As you prepare to navigate the future, remember that strategic success is not a destination; it is a continuous journey of growth, learning, and adaptation. Embrace the changes ahead, and equip yourself and your organisation with the tools and mindset needed to thrive.

**Homework:**

Research one emerging technology relevant to your industry and write a brief report on its potential impact on your organisation's strategy.

Identify two consumer behaviour trends affecting your business. Create an action plan on how your organisation can adapt to meet these changing expectations.

By engaging in these exercises, you will deepen your understanding of future trends in strategic success and develop actionable strategies for navigating the challenges and opportunities that lie ahead. In the next chapter, we will explore the importance of continuous improvement and innovation as cornerstones of lasting success.

# CHAPTER 10: PERSONAL BRANDING FOR STRATEGIC SUCCESS

In today's interconnected world, personal branding is more important than ever. It shapes how others perceive you, influences your professional relationships, and can significantly impact your career success. In this chapter, we will explore the concept of personal branding, its significance in achieving strategic success, and actionable steps to build and maintain a powerful personal brand.

# UNDERSTANDING PERSONAL BRANDING

At its core, personal branding is the process of defining and promoting yourself as a brand. It involves articulating your values, skills, and unique qualities to create a memorable and authentic image. Personal branding is not merely about self-promotion; it's about establishing credibility and building trust with others.

**Why Personal Branding Matters:**

**Differentiation:** In a competitive job market, a strong personal brand helps you stand out. It allows you to showcase your unique strengths and experiences that set you apart from others in your field.

**Influence:** A well-crafted personal brand can enhance your credibility and authority. When people recognize your expertise, they are more likely to seek your opinion, collaborate with you, or refer you to others.

**Opportunities:** Personal branding can open doors to new opportunities. Whether it's landing a new job, gaining clients, or securing speaking engagements, a strong brand can make you a sought-after candidate in your industry.

**Networking:** A solid personal brand creates a lasting impression on your connections. When people remember you positively, they are more likely to engage with you and recommend you to others.

# DEFINING YOUR PERSONAL BRAND

Before you can promote your personal brand, you need to understand what it is. Here's how to define your personal brand effectively:

**Identify Your Values:** Your personal brand should reflect your core values. What principles guide your decisions and actions? Understanding your values will help you communicate authentically and connect with others who share similar beliefs.

**Exercise:** Create a list of your top five values. Reflect on how these values influence your professional life and decisions.

**Assess Your Skills and Strengths:** Take stock of your skills, talents, and experiences. What are you passionate about? What do you excel at? This self-assessment will provide insight into what makes you unique.

**Exercise:** List your top three skills and strengths. Seek feedback from colleagues or mentors to identify areas where you may have overlooked your strengths.

**Understand Your Audience:** Consider who you want to reach with your personal brand. Are you targeting potential employers, clients, or industry peers? Understanding your audience will help you tailor your messaging and approach.

**Exercise:** Create a profile of your ideal audience. What are their interests, challenges, and needs? How can you address these in your branding efforts?

# CRAFTING YOUR PERSONAL BRAND MESSAGE

Once you have a clear understanding of your values, skills, and audience, it's time to craft your personal brand message. This message should encapsulate who you are and what you stand for. Here are key elements to consider:

**Elevator Pitch:** Develop a concise elevator pitch that summarises your personal brand. This should include your name, what you do, and what makes you unique. Your pitch should be engaging and easy to remember.

**Exercise:** Write a 30-second elevator pitch that highlights your skills and what you bring to the table. Practice delivering it confidently and authentically.

**Consistency:** Ensure that your personal brand message is consistent across all platforms. From your resume to your social media profiles, your message should reflect your identity and values cohesively.

**Exercise:** Review your online presence. Do your profiles on LinkedIn, Twitter, and other platforms convey a consistent brand message? Make necessary adjustments to align your profiles.

**Storytelling:** Storytelling is a powerful tool in personal branding. Share your experiences, challenges, and achievements in a way that resonates with your audience. Authentic stories create connections and help others relate to you.

**Exercise:** Write a short narrative about a pivotal moment in your career. Focus on what you learned and how it shaped your professional journey. Use this story as part of your branding efforts.

# BUILDING YOUR PERSONAL BRAND ONLINE

In today's digital age, an online presence is essential for personal branding. Here are effective strategies to build your personal brand online:

**Leverage Social Media:** Social media platforms are powerful tools for building and promoting your personal brand. Choose platforms that align with your audience and industry, such as LinkedIn, Twitter, or Instagram.

**Exercise:** Create a content calendar for your social media posts. Plan to share insights, articles, and experiences that showcase your expertise and values.

**Create Valuable Content:** Sharing valuable content is a great way to establish authority in your field. Write articles, blog posts, or create videos that provide insights, tips, or solutions to common challenges in your industry.

**Exercise:** Set a goal to publish a piece of content each month that showcases your knowledge and expertise. Promote it on your social media channels to increase visibility.

**Engage with Your Audience:** Building a personal brand is not just about self-promotion; it's also about engaging with others. Respond to comments, participate in discussions, and show genuine interest in your audience.

**Exercise:** Dedicate time each week to engage with your audience on social media. Comment on posts, answer questions, and build relationships with your connections.

**Networking:** Attend industry events, webinars, and workshops to connect with others in your field. Networking allows you to share your brand message and learn from others.

**Exercise:** Set a goal to attend at least one networking event per month. Prepare your elevator pitch and be open to meeting new people.

# MAINTAINING YOUR PERSONAL BRAND

Building a personal brand is not a one-time effort; it requires ongoing maintenance and adaptation. Here are some tips for sustaining your brand:

**Stay Authentic:** Authenticity is the cornerstone of a successful personal brand. Be true to yourself and ensure your actions align with your values and message. People are drawn to genuine individuals.

**Exercise:** Regularly reflect on your actions and decisions. Are they in line with your personal brand? Adjust your approach if you find discrepancies.

**Seek Feedback:** Regularly seek feedback from peers, mentors, and trusted colleagues. Constructive feedback can help you identify areas for improvement and reinforce your brand.

**Exercise:** Create a feedback loop by asking colleagues for input on your branding efforts. Use their insights to refine your message and approach.

**Evolve Your Brand:** As you grow and develop, so should your personal brand. Don't be afraid to adapt your message as your career progresses or as industry trends change.

**Exercise:** Schedule time once a year to review and update your personal brand strategy. Reflect on your accomplishments and set new goals.

**Stay Current:** Keep up with industry trends, news, and changes that could impact your brand. Staying informed allows you to remain relevant and position yourself as a thought leader.

**Exercise:** Subscribe to industry publications and set aside time each week to read articles and reports. Share insights with your audience to reinforce your expertise.

# THE IMPACT OF PERSONAL BRANDING ON STRATEGIC SUCCESS

In conclusion, personal branding is a vital component of strategic success. By defining your brand, crafting a compelling message, building an online presence, and maintaining authenticity, you can position yourself as a leader in your field. A strong personal brand enhances your credibility, opens doors to new opportunities, and fosters meaningful connections.

As you move forward, remember that personal branding is an ongoing journey. Embrace the process, be open to learning, and continuously adapt your brand to reflect your growth and evolution. Your personal brand is not just about what you achieve; it's about the impact you have on others and the legacy you leave behind.

**Homework:**

Create your personal branding statement that reflects your values, skills, and what you want to be known for.

Develop a social media strategy to promote your personal brand. Outline what content you will share and how you will engage with your audience.

By actively engaging in these exercises, you will take significant steps toward enhancing your personal brand and achieving strategic success. In the next chapter, we will summarise key concepts from this book and provide actionable steps to implement what you've learned in your journey toward strategic success.

# CONCLUSION: YOUR PATH TO STRATEGIC SUCCESS

As we draw to the end of our journey through "Rise to the Top: Master the Art of Strategic Success," it's essential to reflect on the key concepts we've explored and how they intertwine to create a robust framework for achieving success in both personal and professional realms.

# RECAP OF KEY CONCEPTS

Throughout this book, we delved into various facets of strategic success, from understanding what it truly means to cultivate a strategic mindset. Each chapter was designed to build upon the previous one, creating a comprehensive understanding of the strategic process:

**Understanding Strategic Success**: We defined what strategic success entails—it's more than just achieving goals; it's about aligning your actions with your values, vision, and long-term aspirations.

**The Foundation of Strategy**: We established the fundamental principles of strategy, including the importance of setting clear objectives and the role of research and analysis in informed decision-making.

**Cultivating a Strategic Mindset**: We discussed the necessity of developing a mindset that embraces change, innovation, and resilience, emphasising that adaptability is key in an ever-evolving landscape.

**Crafting a Winning Strategy**: We explored the step-by-step process of creating a strategic plan, highlighting the significance of clarity, focus, and aligning resources with your strategic goals.

**Execution: Turning Strategy into Action**: We learned that even the best strategies require effective execution. This involves mobilising your team, overcoming resistance, and ensuring that everyone is aligned and accountable.

**Measuring Success and Adapting**: Success is not a one-time event but a continuous journey. We emphasised the importance of tracking your progress, analysing outcomes, and being willing to pivot when necessary.

**Building a Strategic Team**: We recognized that no one achieves success alone. A strong, strategic team enhances collaboration and brings diverse perspectives that can drive innovation and growth.

**Navigating Challenges and Obstacles**: Every journey comes with hurdles. We discussed strategies to anticipate and overcome challenges, turning obstacles into opportunities for learning and growth.

**Future Trends in Strategic Success**: We examined emerging trends that are shaping the future of strategy, including technological advancements and shifts in consumer behaviour, highlighting the importance of staying informed and adaptable.

**Personal Branding for Strategic Success**: We concluded with a deep dive into personal branding, understanding how your personal brand can enhance your strategic initiatives and build trust and influence in your field.

# THE IMPORTANCE OF TAKING ACTION

Understanding these concepts is merely the beginning; the real transformation occurs when you put this knowledge into action. Each chapter included practical exercises designed to help you apply the concepts discussed. As you move forward, remember that success is not a destination but a continuous journey of learning, adaptation, and growth.

**Action Steps to Consider**:

**Set Clear Goals**: Take the time to define your strategic goals. What do you want to achieve in the short term and long term? Make sure these goals align with your values and vision.

**Develop a Strategic Plan**: Outline the steps you need to take to reach these goals. Consider resources, timelines, and potential obstacles.

**Embrace a Growth Mindset**: Cultivate a mindset that embraces challenges, learns from failures, and seeks opportunities for improvement.

**Engage Your Team**: Share your vision with your team and involve them in the strategic planning process. Their insights and perspectives can provide valuable input that enhances the overall strategy.

**Monitor Progress**: Regularly review your progress toward your goals. What's working? What's not? Be willing to adapt your strategies based on what you learn.

# THE POWER OF CONNECTION

As you embark on your journey toward strategic success, remember that connection is key. Surround yourself with a network of supportive individuals who share your values and aspirations. Engage with mentors, peers, and even those outside your field to gain new perspectives and insights.

In today's world, collaboration is essential. By building relationships and fostering open communication, you create an environment conducive to success. Remember that every interaction is an opportunity to learn, grow, and expand your horizons.

# A CALL TO CONTINUOUS LEARNING

Strategic success is not a one-time achievement; it requires ongoing commitment to learning and self-improvement. Stay curious, seek knowledge, and be open to new experiences. Attend workshops, read books, and participate in networking events to continue expanding your skill set and understanding of your industry.

The landscape of business and strategy is constantly evolving. Being adaptable and proactive in your learning will ensure that you remain relevant and equipped to navigate the future with confidence.

# EMBRACE YOUR JOURNEY

In conclusion, your journey toward strategic success is uniquely yours. Embrace the challenges, celebrate your victories, and learn from your experiences. The insights and skills you have gained throughout this book are tools to help you rise to the top in your personal and professional life.

Remember, success is not just about reaching a destination; it's about the growth and development you experience along the way. So take action, cultivate your strategic mindset, build your personal brand, and most importantly, believe in yourself and your abilities.

You have the power to shape your future and make a meaningful impact in your chosen path. Now, go forth and master the art of strategic success!

www.ingramcontent.com/pod-product-compliance
Lightning Source LLC
Chambersburg PA
CBHW050312230526
45471CB00005B/2145